Sam Upton

W. A Chamatte

J. B. Kunduma.

Rev H. A. MaWa

S. July Maya

[illegible signature]

B. Kamowa

S. Chilokoteni Box 117 Karonga.

Booker P. K. Banda BOX 745 LILONGWE (the man with beards)

M. T. KACHASO UAMA BOX 177, ZOMBA.

Bro. H. BADUYA

Bro B. Alifeyo Phiri

Ruben L. Nkhata

M Malekano

Marlyn Upton Malinda Upton

MALAWI
THE WARM HEART OF AFRICA

Photographs
and Art Direction:
Hanns Reich

Text:
Juliet Clough

HANNS REICH VERLAG · MUNICH

Printed in Germany by Dr. C. Wolf & Sohn KG, Munich – Lithographs by Repro-Fuchs, Salzburg.
ISBN 3-87668-909-0

FOREWORD

What pleases me much about this collection of beautiful photographs is that no arm of my Government was involved in its production. It is the exclusive work of a clearly talented gentleman who decided to share with others, through photography, the enjoyment of being in Malaŵi.
I am particularly happy that our guest was able to capture vivid images of my women. Why? Because in this country, women have always participated, and still do participate, in our political, economic and social development. One of the gratifying aspects of our contemporary history is the role the women have played in our struggle for independence. As for the post-independence era, many of our visitors are pleasantly surprised when they learn that we have the largest number of lady Members of Parliament in Africa. Our women are involved in every sector of the economy. We have, for example, professional ladies in the fields of agriculture, education, law, medicines and veterinary services.
One of the most popular attractions in this country is Lake Malaŵi, Africa's third largest lake. Its blue water and beautiful beaches are an invitation to any visitor. To facilitate the enjoyment of the visitors to the lake, my Government has embarked on the establishment of modern hotels and improvement of access roads. As a result, not only our guests but my people as well can enjoy their time at the lake.
Man has a past, a present and a future. The three eras are inter-related and indeed influence each other.
During the past twenty years of our existence as a sovereign state I have guided our Nation to prosperity. This is primarily due to what my people have done in the field of agriculture. As a result, they have not only enough to eat but they have surplus to export.
As I look to the futute, I have a vision of our present achievements getting even better. I am certain that future generations of Malaŵians will continue to enjoy more surplus of food, and therefore of better shelter and clothing.
And this is what is deep in my heart when I plan the future of my people, of their children and of the generations to come.

Dr. H. KAMUZU BANDA, Life President

Malawi – the word means, literally, fire flames and is associated with some of the most ancient sacred sites in the country. Like so much that explains modern Malawi, its very name has its roots deep in a tradition which links the people and the land, the life of the spirit with that of the seasons. It is a reminder of a people who lived in the reflected light of a great lake and whose use of fire, both ritual and practical, bound the yearly cycle of heat and rain to the spiritual and physical changes in the human life cycle.

A little, landlocked country in the heart of East Central Africa, Malawi is almost one-fifth water. Its vast lake, southernmost in the chain of the great Rift Valley waters, is 580 km long, the third largest in Africa, and is linked through the Shire River to the Zambezi and the sea. The country is shaped roughly like a dagger or hand-axe, its southern blade sheathed deep in Mozambique, its northern handle bordered on the west by Zambia and to the north and east by Tanzania. But it is Malawi's unique assemblage of physical environments rather than its political boundaries which have determined the character of the country today.

Malawi's borders enclose a variety of terrain unparalleled in this part of Africa. Dominated by the Rift Valley, the country includes an extensive area of the high interior Central African plateau to the west and south. To the north, steep, often precipitous escarpments form the edge of the rift, whose walls plunge with hardly a break sheer into the water and below. The high table land to the north west of the lake reaches its peak at 2,500 m on the beautiful, rolling grasslands of the Nyika Plateau and continues south along the forested Viphya mountains for half the length of the lake. Rich alluvial farmlands stretch along the lakeshore all the way south of Nkhata Bay. Between the Viphya and Dedza is an extensive plain some 900 m high, which gives way at the south end of the lake to the tropically hot, low-lying Shire Valley with its sugar and cotton fields. In the Shire Highlands to the east of the rift in southern Malawi, at an elevation of 600 to 900 m, the climate is cool and stimulating, with heavy rainfall in the summer. The beautiful plateaux of Zomba Mountain (2087 m) and Mulanje, at 3000 m the highest mountain in Central Africa, dominate this area, their dramatic rocky outcrops clothed with cedar and pine forests and, in season, with fields of wild orchids and gladioli. Both the red soils of the plateaux and the black soils of the lowlands are highly fertile and once teemed with wildlife, whose descendents still roam the country's national parks, while Lake Malawi and its smaller satellites are a valuable source of fish.

It all adds up to one of the most generous landscapes in Central Africa, and consequently one of the most densely populated – a green basin which has gradually collected and mingled the incoming streams and trickles of many African peoples and called them its own. As far back as the archaeologist's spade can reach, Malawi has been a place from whence travellers, once arrived from less hospitable environments, saw no reason to move on. Despite its comparatively small size, Malawi today supports a population of more than 6½ million, considerably greater than that of her much larger neighbour, Zambia, and almost as great as that of Zimbabwe.

The earliest traces of human habitation in Malawi are some heavy duty axes, cleavers and scrapers, possibly as much as 100,000 years old, which were excavated at Early Stone Age sites near Karonga and Dedza. No trace has yet been found of their users. The more specialised and precisely flaked tools of the Middle Stone Age, dating from between 50,000 and 10,000 years ago, are found all over the country. The first Malawians known to archaeologists date from the Late Stone Age. Skeletons found in a rock shelter on Hora Mountain, near Mzimba, and in another on Fingira Hill on the Nyika Plateau, the latter some 3,530 to 3,350 years old, belonged to a small-statured race described as exhibiting Bushman and Negroid characteristics. Later Stone Age man in Malawi lived by hunting and gathering his food. He knew how to use bone and sinew as well as stone and was the first to decorate his home with the type of schematic paintings that can still be seen today in rock shelters such as those at Chencherere. Oral tradition still remembers the *Batwa* or Little People as their more sophisticated successors remembered the diminutive race which they gradually replaced. It is a folklore theme that is popular in many parts of the world. One story indicates that the *Batwa* were sensitive about their size. Meeting a stranger their first question was: "Where did you see me?", the only acceptable answer being a tactful: "I saw you from far away".

Early in the first millenium after Christ a wave of new people, Bantu speakers, bringing with them a knowledge of iron working, farming, pottery and cattle-keeping came fanning southwards and eastwards through Africa. Sometime during the 3rd century AD these newcomers arrived in the Malawi area and quickly colonised the lakeshore and the major river valleys, living in settled villages, practising a truly mixed economy, interacting with and gradually overtaking their hunter-gatherer predecessors (though hunting itself has never gone out of fashion). Sometime after 1200 AD a new wave of Bantu immigrations arrived from the north and east and for the next few

Blacksmiths at work in 1860. Ironworking remained a traditional skill in remote areas as late as the 1940s.

centuries Malawi was peopled by small, localised tribes, each owing allegiance to a chief who rendered religious, judicial and military services to his people. Modern Chewa tradition holds that their first recognisable ancestors migrated from south eastern Zaire. On reaching the southern end of the lake they rapidly expanded their territory and established themselves as rulers. The beginning of the 16th century saw the emergence of the Maravi empire, a loose but powerful confederation of states which was finally to encompass the greater part of eastern Zambia, central and southern Malawi and northern Mozambique. In their heyday, the Maravi were the most renowned power-brokers north of the Zambezi; even the Portuguese, who by this time had begun to tap the rich trading potential of the area, often recruited Maravi warriors for their own campaigns. But by the mid 18th century, the Maravi empire was in decline, undermined by revolts, religious secessions and the pressures of contact with the outside world, though a common linguistic and cultural unity still survives among the disparate groups to which it gave rise. The Chewa, Mang'anja and Nyanja groupings are still reflected in clan names and their localities today.

Meanwhile a forceful new people was making its presence felt in the south. The Yao, extending their long-distance trading contacts from the Swahili coast brought their guns with them, seeking not only ivory, skins, copper and finally slaves, but political control as well. The Yao established themselves around Blantyre, Zomba and the south end of the lake, gradually introducing aspects of Swahili culture which are still much in evidence today. From the 1840s a number of Swahili came too. The powerful trading depot established by the Jumbe of Nkhotakota on the lakeshore, for example, was a direct extension of the Omani Arabs' commercial empire at Zanzibar. Koranic schools were opened and substantial groups converted in the 1890s to Islam, still the predominant religion in these areas.

With the 19th century began the blackest period in Malawi's history, the zenith of the slave trade, when countless thousands of wretched individuals rounded up from villages deep in the African interior made the long journey to the trading entrepots on the lake, Karonga, Nkhotakota and Mponda's (near Mangochi). From thence Arab dhows would convey them across the lake for the last stage of the forced trail which would end in the coastal slave markets of Kilwa and Zanzibar. By 1870 it was estimated that Nkhotakota and Mponda's each had an annual turnover of about 10,000 slaves. The

David Livingstone noticed the local techniques of ridging and subsoil burning in 1863. "I meant to teach these people agriculture" remarked his friend, Bishop Mackenzie, the first missionary settler in Malawi, "but I now see they know far more about it than I do".

accounts of early explorers paint a horrifying picture of the brutality of these caravans, the people yoked together like animals, loaded with ivory, the sick or weak beaten, shot or left to die by the roadside.

The 19th century saw other, alarming arrivals. Far to the south in Natal, the rise of a section of Chaka's warlike Zulu nation led to the migration northward of the Ngoni, who broke away under Zwangendaba. They crossed the Zambezi in 1835, accumulating cattle and dependents, and after extensive wanderings and raidings established several kingdoms, notably between

Livingstone's steamer, the Ma Robert, with a foreground of hippopotamus traps and a victim. Poisoned spikes, set on the ends of heavy wooden beams, fell at the tread of frightened hippos, providing a feast for the village.

Dedza and Ntcheu and in the northern hills near Ekwendeni, skirmishing as far as the lakeshore for women and food supplies. Eventually the much feared Ngoni intermarried and settled down, though traces of their language, and their strong traditions of cattle keeping and martial dancing still characterise Ngoni areas today.

The arrival of David Livingstone, the famous Scottish missionary-explorer, in 1859 was to herald a whole new age for Malawi. Baffled on his second expedition into the African interior by the Cabora Bassa rapids on the Zambezi he turned his small launch, the 'Ma Robert', up a tributary, the Shire, travelling as far as the cataracts at the foot of the Shire Highlands and continuing on foot to obtain his first glimpse of the rumoured lake. In 1861 he returned to launch his first exploration of Lake Malawi, leaving a small party of Anglican missionaries at Magomero. The British presence in Malawi had arrived, though this first settlement was soon abandoned. Livingstone's accounts of the slave trade were to inspire the wave of missionary activity which was to follow him to Malawi, but he also noticed the flourishing cotton fields and the great agricultural potential of the area: "I go back to Africa to try to make an open path for commerce and Christianity" he told British audiences. He also left a political legacy in the shape of a small band of Makololo porters who had accompanied him from Western Zambia and

View of Cape Maclear in 1877, the pioneer Livingstonia settlement, and the mission steamer Ilala.

whom he had left, equipped with guns, settled in the far south near Chikwawa after his first visit to the area. The Makololo's close alliance with the British by the time of the partition of Africa in the 1880s caused the missionaries to demand that this Makololo area of their influence should be kept free from what would otherwise have been Portuguese control; hence Malawi's comma-shaped southern tail.

Livingstone crossed his "lake of stars" once again on his final journey in search of the source of the Nile. He died in Zambia in 1873 and two years later the Free Church of Scotland's Livingstonia Mission was established at Cape Maclear in his memory. Missionary graves and mounds where buildings once stood testify to disease, death and the difficulties of making converts in an area already culturally linked to the Swahili coast through trade; the mission soon moved its headquarters to Bandawe, and finally settled far to the north in 1894 at present day Livingstonia.

The Church of Scotland arrived in the south in 1876 to found a station that was to develop into the town of Blantyre. Soon a liberated slave settlement grew up on the slopes of nearby Ndirande Mountain. Where Christianity led the way, commerce was not slow to follow. In 1878 the African Lakes Company was formed by the brothers John and Frederic Moir as a means of introducing legitimate trade to replace the horrors of slavery. Their Blantyre depot, Mandala House (the company was given the local name for John Moir's spectacles), survives today as the oldest building in the country. By 1884 the African Lakes Company had prospered enough to open up a new trading post in the far north at Karonga and from the mid 1880s planters and traders of various nationalities arrived to acquire land from local chiefs. In 1885 the Universities Mission to Central Africa (U.M.C.A.) returned to base themselves on Likoma Island where they later built a magnificent cathedral. In retaining a firm hold on Likoma, mission influence was once again to reserve

for Malawi a portion of land which, geographically, was part of the Portuguese sphere of influence. Soon the lake was awash with little steamers, plying up and down in the cause of Christianity and hard cash. A British Consul had been appointed in 1883 and in 1891 the country was declared a British Protectorate, partly to counter Portuguese expansionist ambitions. The first Commissioner of Nyasaland, as Malawi was then called, was Harry Hamilton Johnston, a small and dapper teetotaller, a gifted naturalist with a vast enthusiasm for work. Johnston made it his business to tackle the slave trade in earnest, ending it north and south by force of arms and finally smashing the Karonga fortress of the powerful trader Mlozi. Johnston left his mark on modern Malawi in the shape of an efficient administrative network, more than 600 km of roads, a system of taxation, a postal service and the beginnings of an army which was to play its part in both World Wars. From the 1890s large amounts of land, particularly in the Shire Highlands, passed into the hands of foreign settlers, who opened up coffee, cotton and tobacco estates, none at first very successful. It was not until the 1930s that today's green carpet of tea began to spread over the slopes around Mulanje and Thyolo. African smallholder farming, now an important part of the agricultural scene, began with the production of food crops for labourers on the estates but quickly expanded, particularly after the First War, with a growth in cotton growing on the lower Shire and in fire-cured tobacco on the Lilongwe plains. One result of the low wages paid by the settlers was that labour became a major export, as thousands of Malawians flocked south to the mines of what was then Rhodesia and South Africa, many, particularly from the north, taking their new mission education to corner the better paid jobs. Labour migration reached a peak in the early 1970s when an estimated 270,000 Malawians were in employment outside the country. The number has dropped sharply to a very few thousand today.
Malawians began to take a hand in their own national destiny in 1915 when the Reverend John Chilembwe, a stern critic of the government, planned an uprising in protest against conditions on European estates. Chilembwe had worked with the radical evangelist missionary Joseph Booth, had studied theology in the United States and had launched his own successful church, the Providence Industrial Mission whose site can still be seen at Chiradzulu. The uprising was quickly quashed and Chilembwe shot dead. He is now regarded as the first Malawian martyr to the cause of African freedom. Throughout the 1920s and 30s the churches and Native Associations formed a network of contacts through which educated protest could be voiced, though with little

real effect. In 1944 the Nyasaland African Congress (N.A.C.) was formed as the first indigenous political party. With the imposition in 1953 of the hated Federation of Rhodesia and Nyasaland, the groundswell of rural discontent with colonial agricultural policies was reinforced by increasingly militant demands from the young radicals in Congress for self government and universal suffrage. Only a leader was lacking and in 1958 the return of Dr. Hastings Kamuzu Banda at the invitation of the NAC to lead the party, after nearly 40 years abroad, brought matters to a head. The campaigning of Dr. Banda and his lieutenants led to a series of clashes with colonial officials and the following year a state of emergency was declared, the party banned, its leaders and nearly 1,000 supporters arrested and 52 Africans killed. In 1960 Dr. Banda was released by the British Colonial Secretary and invited to talks in London; the August elections of the following year brought the new Malawi Congress Party a sweeping victory. The country attained full self-government in 1963 with Dr. Banda as Prime Minister and on July 6th 1964 the Protectorate of Nyasaland became the fully independent state of Malawi. In 1966 the country took on the status of a republic within the British Commonwealth, with Dr. Banda elected as President. He became Life President in 1971 and has since ruled the country with a firm hand, personally approving the members of the National Assembly who are elected from a list of candidates provided by local committees of the Party.

Much has been achieved in the years since Independence. Despite a population increase of 60 per cent in the years between 1966 and 1983, less than 10 per cent of the populace lives in towns, the vast majority of the rest are hardworking farmers, growing enough maize, cassava, millet, sorghum, groundnuts, rice, pulses, coffee, fruit and vegetables to feed their families as well as producing enough surplus to stock the colourful marketplaces up and down the country.

Malawi is now largely self-sufficient and since Independence there has been a major expansion in cash crops as well as foodstuffs. Any surpluses produced by villagers are bought by the Agricultural Development and Marketing Board (ADMARC) which sets up more than 700 temporary markets throughout the country each year. ADMARC also provides farmers with fertilisers, assistance and advice, runs a canning factory, exports agricultural products and is actively engaged in livestock production. With the expansion of commercial agriculture there has been a marked increase in African-owned estates, particularly in the tobacco lands of the Central Region and the north. Tobacco is Malawi's main export crop, about 40,000 tonnes of it, a figure second only to Zimbabwe's in terms of total African output. Flue-cured and burley tobacco is grown on the big estates, fire or sun/air cured is reserved for smallholders. The United Kingdom is Malawi's main customer, though tobacco is exported to 50 other countries.

Tea, Malawi's "green gold", has been grown on the gently undulating uplands around Mulanje and Thyolo for decades and is the country's second export crop, with cane sugar, grown on vast estates in the Lower Shire Valley and on the lakeshore near Nkhotakota coming next and coffee, rice, groundnuts and cotton, cashew, tung (a high-quality tree nut oil used in paints and varnishes), macadamia and rubber all taking lesser places as foreign-exchange earners. Much of the country's cotton goes to the David Whitehead factory in Blantyre where the gaily printed Chitenje cloth, the graceful national dress of Malawi and much of Central Africa is made.

Private and government investment from the West has been welcomed and a favourable investment climate created through the country's good record of political and monetary stability. The Life President has done much to ensure that Malawians play a leading role in the economy, partly by establishing African owned corporations (the multi-faceted Press Holdings is his own creation). Today Malawi brews its own beer and patent medicines, weaves its own cotton and blankets, processes its own grain, sugar and vegetable oils, makes its own shoes, spaghetti, stationery, bricks and cement and ties its own fishing flies. The government-owned Malawi Development Corporation exists to promote new enterprises by combining local potential and know-how with outside expertise and investment.

The 'wild and not unpleasant music of the Marimba' or giant xylophone, heard by David Livingstone in 1859 in the Lower Shire Valley, is still popular entertainment in southern Malawian villages.

Transport, agriculture and education have been primary targets for development since Independence and international organisations have largely replaced foreign governments as the most important source of foreign aid. Modern market places, schools, clinics and community halls around the country are the tangible results of current rural development schemes. Roads and rail links are systematically improving.

Music and dance, the chief cultural expression of the Malawian people, have for long been political vehicles as well as a natural part of any celebration. A traveller passing through a country village in the Nsanje district might well find himself listening to the sound of a huge wood and gourd xylophone, nearly 3 m long and played by three men at once, while the villagers prepare for a wedding or a Party meeting by working through the symbolic figures of a complicated dance. In the north Ingoma, the war dance of the Ngoni, still enlivens public events. Other military dances, like the Yao Beni, and Malipenga from Likoma Island are partly relics of World War I, first danced in the prisoner of war camps and mining compounds of the '20s. The dancers dress in smart white or khaki uniforms and are organised into semi-military teams, complete with officers, doctors and judges.

For the visitor it is the Malawian people themselves, whether encountered over a purchase or a puncture, in a simple holiday hotel, a busy town or quiet village whose invariable courtesy, friendliness and helpfulness have truly earned their country its reputation as "the warm heart of Africa".

Those interested in photography may like to know that the photographs in this book were taken with Nikon cameras on Kodachrome and Ektachrome films. – The engravings in the introduction are reproduced from the following books: David Livingstone: "Narrative of an Expedition to the Zambesi and its Tributaries" (pages 7, 8, 9, 13) and J. F. Elton: "The Lakes and Mountains of Eastern and Central Africa" (page 10).

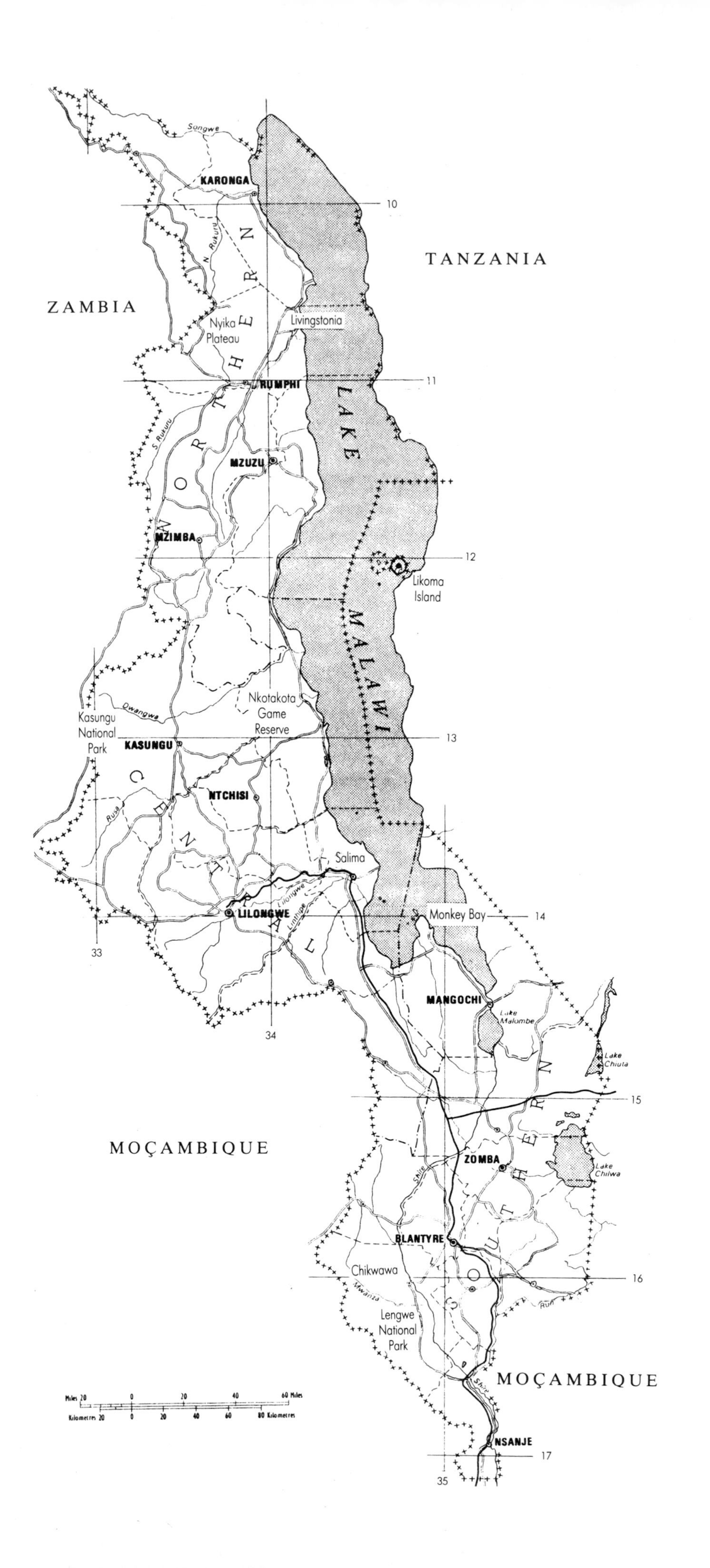

TANZANIA
ZAMBIA
MOÇAMBIQUE
MOÇAMBIQUE
LAKE
MALAWI
N O R T H E R N
C E N T R A L
S O U T H E R N
KARONGA
Livingstonia
Nyika
Plateau
RUMPHI
MZUZU
MZIMBA
Likoma
Island
Nkotakota
Game
Reserve
Kasungu
National
Park
KASUNGU
NTCHISI
Salima
LILONGWE
Monkey Bay
MANGOCHI
Lake
Malombe
Lake
Chiuta
Lake
Chilwa
ZOMBA
BLANTYRE
Chikwawa
Lengwe
National
Park
NSANJE
Songwe
Shire
10
11
12
13
14
15
16
17
33
34
35
Miles 20 0 20 40 60 Miles
Kilometres 20 0 20 40 60 80 Kilometres

Malawi National Anthem

Mulungu dalitsani Malaŵi,	God bless our land of Malawi,
Mumsunge mtendere;	Keep her a land of peace;
Gonjetsani adani onse:	Put down each and every enemy:
Njala, nthenda, umphawi;	Hunger, disease and poverty;
Lunzitsani mitima yathu,	Join all our hearts as one,
Kuti tisaope;	Thus we are free from fear;
Dalitsani mtsogoleri nd'ife,	Bless our leader and every one of us,
Ndi mayi Malaŵi.	And mother Malawi.
Chichewa	*English translation*

His Excellency the Life President of the Republic of Malawi, Ngwazi Dr. H. Kamuzu Banda, often appears among his people.

Gaily uniformed Mbumba, members of the League of Malawi Women, crowd the Life President's public appearances.

4 Kamuzu Stadium in Blantyre, packed out for a state occasion. Regional dances, military displays and football matches are standard entertainment during official functions. – 5 · As always, there is red-carpet treatment for the guest of honour.

The songs and dances of praise of the M'bumba, for whom the President is their special guardian, deal mainly with the history of independence and the themes of current development and are taught to all schoolgirls. The ladies, led by the Official Hostess, Mama C. Tamanda Kadzamira, dance in the grounds of Sanjika Palace.

8 · The kachere or wild fig tree under which Dr. Banda learnt the alphabet from a Free Church of Scotland missiontrained evangelist near his birthplace at Mtunthama. He was later to walk more than 1,600 km to the Republic of South Africa in search of further education. In telling contrast nearby is – 9 · Kamuzu Academy, Malawi's lavishly-endowed new grammar school.

9

A strong educational tradition dates back to the 1880s, when the first Free Church of Scotland missionaries and their followers began to establish a network of schools that was to give the Malawians an enviable reputation.

Kamuzu Academy, a special project of the Life President's, built in his home district near Kasungu, is the fulfilment of a dream. Here the classics are taught in the atmosphere of a British public school to children for whom no expense, in terms of staffing, library, sporting and other facilities has been spared.

11

11, 12 · The Great Hall of the University of Malawi, Chancellor College, Zomba, a gift of the Life President. Chancellor College provides the university's main acadamic focus. There are three other campuses, the Polytechnic in Blantyre, the Bunda College of Agriculture and the Kamuzu College of Nursing in Lilongwe.

13, 14, 15 · Built on Likoma Island in Lake Malawi, Saint Peter's Cathedral was completed in 1911 by the Universities' Mission to Central Africa. It is an astonishing creation, nearly 100 m long, in granite and anthill mud, with many stained glass windows and gothic details. There is still said to be 100 % literacy among the island's fishing community.

13

14

Over the past century, Christianity has become a deeply-rooted part of the Malawian culture, the legacy of a strong missionary tradition. The Universities' Mission to Central Africa was the first to answer the appeal made by David Livingstone, the famous missionary explorer, for a Christian mission to Central Africa. The Anglican group arrived in 1861 and settled near Blantyre but were soon forced to leave by fever and the failure of several injudicious attempts to interfere with the slave trade. They eventually returned from Zanzibar to settle on Likoma Island. Next to arrive was the Livingstonia Mission of the Free Church of Scotland, under the redoubtable Aberdeen-born Dr. Robert Laws. The missionaries attempted a base on the lake at Cape

Maclear and later at Bandawe, finally settling far to the north on a high plateau overlooking the lake. Here a great training institution, with a hospital, post office, workshops and schools was set up. For generations it sent out educated men to corner the better-paid jobs in mines and offices all over East and Southern Africa, establishing outstations throughout northern Malawi. The Church of Scotland arrived in the south in 1876 and built the imposing church which is now one of the country's most prized monuments. Catholic and Dutch Reformed Church missionaries also established churches and schools in many parts of the country.

16, 17 · "The most wonderful church in Africa". "Ethereal, immaterial . . . it looks as if fairies built it". The raptures of early travellers to Blantyre on first beholding the Church of Saint Michael and All Angels, the first permanent Christian church to be erected between the Zambezi and the Nile, are recorded in a dozen memoirs and biographies. Dedicated in 1891, the church was designed by the Church of Scotland missionary David Clement Scott. Neither Scott nor his team of Malawian builders had had any previous architectural experience. A blend of Latin, Byzantine and Romanesque styles symbolised the missionaries' hope for a uniform African Christianity, free from the petty divisions of Europe.

18 · The Church at Livingstonia was begun in 1916 by Free Church of Scotland missionaries. Situated in the beautiful hill country near the north end of Lake Malawi, this was the third site chosen by the first missionary settlers and named after the explorer David Livingstone.

17

 18

19–22 · Whether your church is mud, brick or simply a patch of shade, Sunday is go-to-meeting day all over Malawi.

23

24

24 · The interior of the mosque in Zomba. – 25 · The new mosque in Limbe. Malawi's predominantly Muslim Asian community do thriving business in the main urban centres of Lilongwe, Blantyre and Zomba. Indians, most of them travelling northwards from the Zambezi, began to trade in Malawi from the 1890s. Islam is also a strong Malawian tradition, particularly in those areas of the south where Yao trading contacts with the coast introduced many aspects of Swahili culture.

26

Ingoma, the famous dance brought from South Africa by warriors of Zulu origin (Ngoni people), who settled in the 19th century, recalls the wars, raids and skirmishings which preceded their settlement in Malawi. Dance is a way of life here, a ceremonious expression of history, religion, politics, custom and the whole range of human experience with its joys and sorrows. There are dances for work as well as war, dances for love and hate, for prosperity and calamity, for medicine and rain, education and initiation. Dance has become an integral part of all celebrations and state occasions. You name it, in Malawi they dance it.

Animal masks and symbolic paintings keep away the spirits of the recently dead. Gule Wamkulu, the Great Dance, the most ancient, mysterious and ritually significant of Malawi's dances, is closely linked with the secret Nyau organisation. Associated with death, witchcraft and initiation, Gule Wamkulu is more than a dance, an expression, too, of deep religious and emotional feelings. Elaborate animal masks may recall an ancient hunter-gatherer people who had turned to agriculture but who still found themselves in conflict with the unpredictable forces of the wild.

28

29

It is auspicious to look solemn for the wedding photograph. A giant kudu horn provides the processional music. After the wedding, the young couple will probably live at the wife's village. With the exception of the patrilineal north, Malawi has a largely matrilineal social structure, which gives key male responsibility in any family to the uncles, brothers and male relatives of the women rather than to their husbands.

Hump-backed zebu cattle graze the fertile *dambos* or water meadows. The gentle sound of iron cow bells is particularly heard in the far north where cattle farming is the traditional livelihood of the Ngonde people.
34 · Malawi's rural water projects are a self-help story envied in many neighbouring countries. Teams of villagers have dug channels many miles long to bring water from rivers or mountain streams to their remote communities.

Stilted stores of woven cane keep each household's maize crop dry and ventilated.
36 · Stripped off the cob, the dried maize is rhythmically pounded to a fine flour called *ufa* to make *nsima,* or maize porridge, the nation's staple dish.

Yao village elder. His Muslim mode of dress, like the mango trees in the background and his square house, is a legacy from the days when his people traded in ivory, copper and slaves with the coastal Arabs.

38 · Fingers flash over the Bawo board. Malawi's great game of calculation is played under village trees, in barbers' queues and office compounds everywhere. Inter-village competition, with goats for wagers, can be fierce.

39

Elephant of the vegetable world, the baobab rings the lakeshore.
42 · As evening falls the children, like children everywhere else, turn to football.

Ridged rows of growing cassava, later spread out for sale in the market offer an alternative menu to maize. 45 · Graphite-decorated pots carry head loads of water over long distances. Cassava needs a lot of soaking before it becomes edible.

43

Wire model toys bowl merrily along urban streets, the special skill of the town child who has access to odd materials. Children are adept improvisers, making toys out of mud, sisal or old plastic containers, anything that happens to come to hand in a waste-not society.

48

49 The shopping centre in Thyolo.

 Lemons today, pineapples, mangoes, or avocados tomorrow. The seasons govern the largesse which overflows market stalls.

53 Fresh or frozen? Department store variety complements home-grown plenty. Canned produce is also exported abroad.

WINES
PAPER GOODS
JUICE
RICE

A chequerboard of P. O. Boxes await addressees' keys.
57 · Sunshine and a spot of shade on the way home.

55

56

60 · Rubber trees yield up their latex on a nothern estate established in 1912. – 58 · Sheets of latex are smoked in a special building. Vizara rubber is both exported and used in local manufacture.

59 · Tea, Malawi's green gold, has been grown on the gently undulating uplands around Thyolo and the skirts of the Mulanje massif for decades, with a major expansion in the 1930s and further growth since Independence. Tea estates today tend to diversify, growing complementary crops such as coffee, macadamia and tung nuts, a policy found to be the most productive response to the land, the seasons and the world commodity markets. Smallholder schemes, established since Independence, enable small farmers to grow both tea and flue-cured tobacco, formerly the preserves of the large estate owners. Tea estates are still owned by expatriate companies but tobacco estates are now largely controlled by Malawians.

58

Malawi remains by design a country of country people, unlike most of her African neighbour-states, where a steady drift to the towns has resulted in growing urban squalor. The patchwork fields of the village smallholder are the true stuff of the land, land which is increasingly producing enough for outside markets as well as feeding families. Rice is widely grown under irrigation in the Shire Valley, on the Zomba plains and along the lake shore.

Vast silos near Lilongwe maintain a strategic reserve which is stored for a year and exported only if the new harvest meets home requirements.

Tobacco, Malawi's top crop, is grown on large estates and on smallholdings. Estate-grown flue-cured and burley tobacco is used by both pipe and cigarette smokers, while the fire or air-cured leaf grown by smallholders is mainly for the pipe smoker. Tobacco auctions attract many buyers from all over the world.

An oil tanker for the lake is assembled at Monkey Bay. The boatyard was established with the help of the West German government.

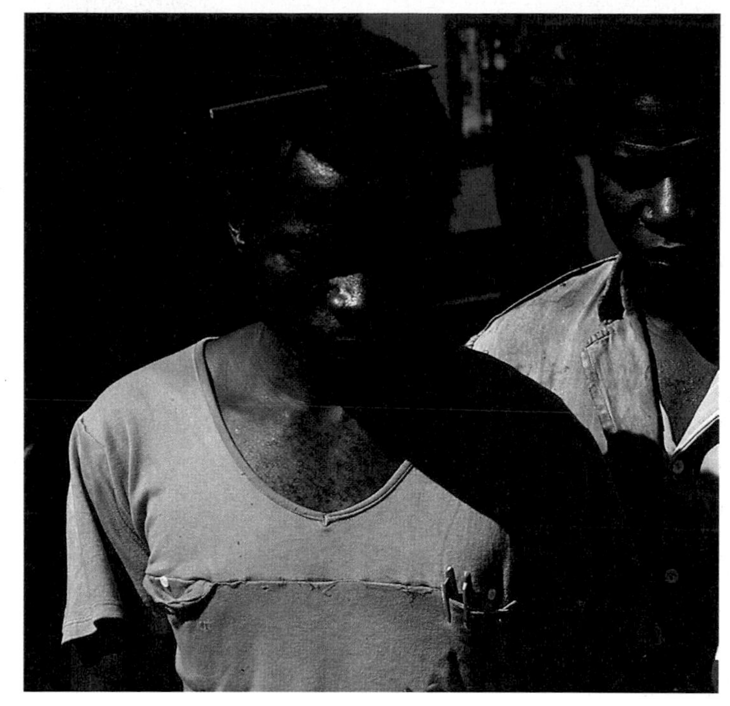

67

68

Delamere house in Blantyre and a cool green spot to rest the eye as the city goes about its business

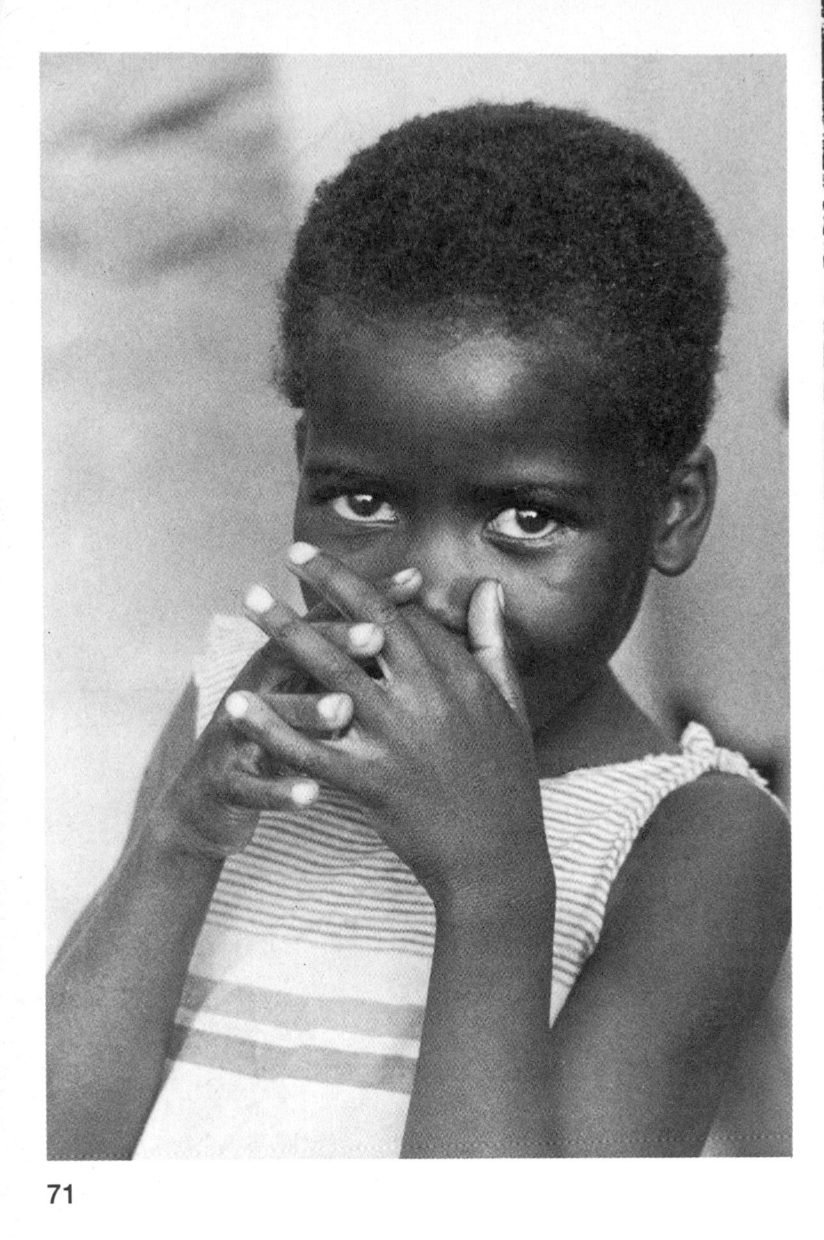

71

Home from the market. Blantyre's suburbs have expanded fast to ring a thriving commercial city.

73 *Mandala House,* the oldest building in Malawi. It was once the trading depot of the African Lakes Company.

The fibrous agave flourishes nearly everywhere in Malawi.

The elderly charm of Malawi's colonial architecture mellows alongside the contemporary in today's citylandscapes. (75 · Zomba – 76 and 77 · Lilongwe)

76

75 77

Contemporary outlines of one of Africa's newest cities. Lilongwe replaced the colonial town of Zomba as capital in 1975. The Reserve Bank of Malawi building is a fascinating example of modern architecture.

Business as usual in the city, whether you are heading for the shops, the office or the commuter bus.

83

Malawi's young capital, Lilongwe, is growing up in a green oasis of carefully planned, lush vegetation.

Doorstep enterprise: verandah or *khonde* tailoring is colourful, effective and cheap – and usually an overnight job.

Garden city explosion of green – it can be a long walk to work. (Lilongwe).

90 · Open-bill stork. –

91 · A group of egret awaiting the swarm of insects escaping from an end-of-season grass burning. – 92 · Roasting maize.

91 92

93 At Mzuzu Airport, the *tambala* cockerel crows for an Independence Day anniversary.

94 The Kamuzu International Airport near Lilongwe is a boost to business and tourism.

96

A weaver nests and a tourist dips in the grounds of a Blantyre hotel. Modern hotels in the remote north, the central capital and the populous south have opened up fresh horizons for travellers, migrants or otherwise.

97

98

99

100

101

100 · And so to Lake Malawi, the vast waterway which covers one-fifth of the total area of the country. A spectacular German-designed corniche road scales the heights above its mountainous northern end, linking this remote area with the rest of the lake shore highway. – 101 · In the water, a rainbow array of rare, mouth-breeding cichlids – many of them unique in the world to their own few hundred metres of shoreline – are a tempting bait for collectors. They also are exported.

103

104 105

M. V. Ilala, successor to Lake Malawi's earliest steamship and named after the place where Livingstone died, regularly travels the 580 km of Aftrica's loveliest waterway. She is attended at every port of call by flotillas of dugout canoes bringing cargoes of dried fish, goats, bicycles and food for passengers, muscovy ducks and sugar cane. Much of the fishing on Lake Malawi is still done from dugout canoes, made from hollowed tree trunks – a craft as old as fishing itself and now nearing the end of its life. Boat building and firewood cutting have taken their toll of the dense forests that used to surround the lake and now the canoe fisherman has to seek his tree as much as 100 km from the shore. The canoe is built in the forest and, failing other transport, dragged on wooden rollers by relays of villagers to its launching. Dugout styles vary up and down the lake and fishermen are adept at handling up to 1000 m of net, 10 m wide, from one canoe. They ride the waves with a pliancy that might well be envied by more sophisticated craft.

107

109

Proud, raucous-voiced fish eagles use their razor-sharp claws to carry off their prey from the surface waters.

On Boadzulu Island a vast colony of white-necked cormorants also compete with the boatmen for fish.

Attended by a flotilla of hopeful pelicans, a fleet of trawlers sets out at dawn to harvest the lake. Caught in a web of air and dappled shade, catches are smoked, sun-dried or otherwise processed for home consumption or export. The lake is a valuable source of fish which, since the advent of the bicycle and now the lorry, are widely transportable.

The ruffled fisheagle is no longer monarch of all he surveys. The hotels on the lakeshore are ideal places for recreation.

115

116 118

As yet truly unspoilt, Lake Malawi's fine golden sands and limpid warm waters offer visitors all the ingredients of ideal holidays.

A shy Nyala and a family of baboons share an evening drink. Observers can do the same in the thatched rondavals of Lifupa Lodge, the human waterhole at Kasungu National Park.

Nature in the raw, with a few creature comforts thrown in: the four main National Parks each has its own speciality to offer. There are few commercialised gimmicks to rub the bloom off these unspoilt Edens. *Kasungu National Park* has an animal population typical of that of the Central African plateau, with its low vegetation and shallow water meadows. Here the elephant is king. At *Liwonde National Park* there are large areas of wetland, an important aquatic bird sanctuary and home to hundreds of protected hippopotami and crocodiles. Bird life is unbelievably rich. There are more than 600 recorded species in the national parks. *Lengwe* has been a reserve since 1928 for the protection of the Nyala antelope, here on the northernmost limit of its territory. A more recent provision of permanent waterholes has brought a dramatic growth in the animal population.

Kasungu National Park

Ancient and modern art. A roadside carver finishes off an ancestral 'family tree'. In rockshelters all over the country, red schematic paintings dating from the Late Stone Age show cryptic circles, grids, loops and ladders, a mysterious code that is still waiting to be broken.

Zomba Plateau.

Bird's eye view from the Ku-Chawe-Inn, perched on the rim of Zomba Plateau. Thousands of square kilometres of Central Africa with its mountains, forests and waters spread out below, pinpricked at night with the lights of countless village fires.

126

127 128

A magnificent 2,087 m. plateau overlooks the little hill town of Zomba. With its pine forests and well stocked trout streams and with its unparalleled views, named respectively after a Queen and an Emperor who were once brought to admire them, this is one of the country's most famous beauty spots. Zomba Plateau's forests are the home of leopards and rare blue monkeys. Its meadows are filled in season with orchids and butterflies. When David Livingstone walked along the Mulunguzi stream in 1859, its boulders and brackenfilled pine woods must have reminded him of his native Scotland.

129

130

Riders from the school of equitation trek through idyllic scenery of the Zomba Plateau.
130 · Thousands of pine seedlings – *pinus patula,* an incomer from Mexico – await transplantation into the mountain forests which supply most of the country's timber needs.

131, 132 · The Mulunguzi Dam was stocked with trout in early colonial times and still provides good sport.

133 Chagwa Dam on Zomba Plateau is a spot for the contemplation of fishermen and picnickers.

Cheaper than tractors and less fussy about difficult terrain, trained oxen undertake much of Malawi's forest logging work.

Mpatamango Gorge. Cataracts on these southern reaches of the Shire River foiled Livingstone's ambition to navigate to the interior along the Zambezi from the sea. Bent bamboo and woven vines take the traveller safely over the torrent. The Shire provides enough hydro eletric power for most of Malawi's domestic needs, with still some to spare for neighbours.

Vistas of flat-topped acacia trees typify areas of virgin forest. Vivid proteas and mango trees make gardens of the wilderness.

138

139

140

Her geographical position has secured for Malawi a potpourri of African flora. A rich diversity of habitat includes montane forest and grassland, tropical rain forest and high and low altitude brachystegia woodland.

Nyika Plateau

The champagne sting of morning on the roof of the world; billow after billow, the colours shift on Nyika's blowing grasslands from tawny gold to mauve, pink and indigo. Its hollows are patched with forest greens, its meadows flamboyand with alpine flowers. This magnificent skyscape, nearly 2,500 metres high, is home to innumerable antelope, zebras, leopards and mountain birds.

144

142

143 145

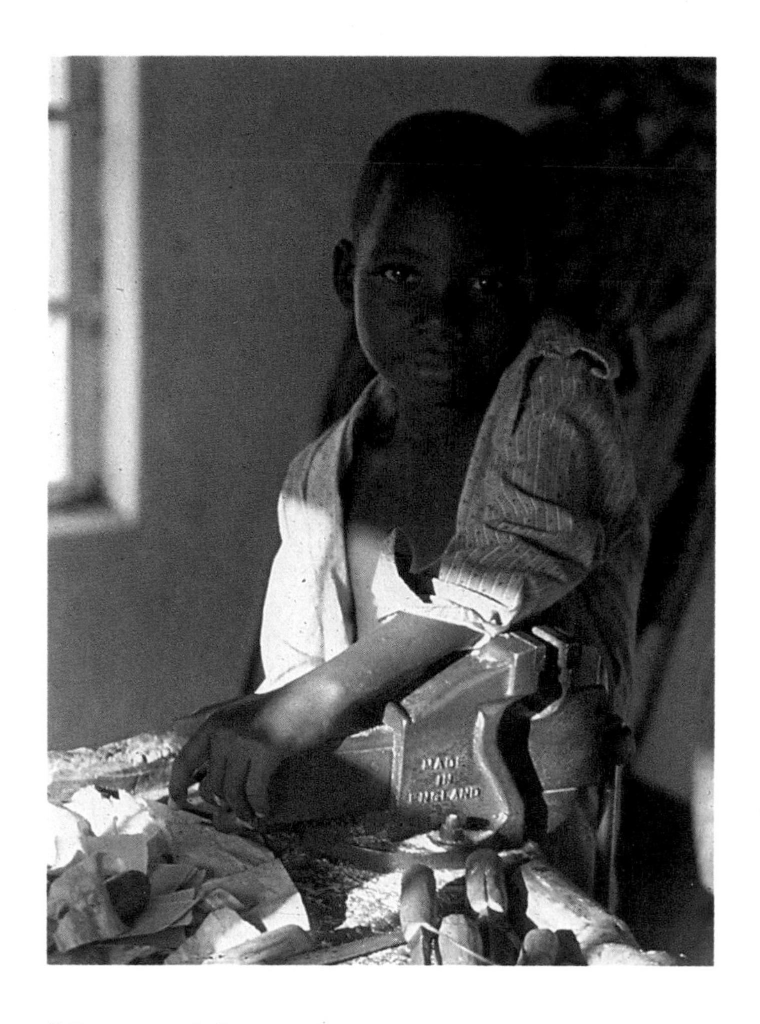

Like a seed, I was sown;
Like a germinating seed I was born;
Life and the world I found;
Like nutrients, in the roots of life I flow;
Like the leaves awaiting their nutritional needs,
The future awaits my arrival;
For tomorrow I strive,
The future . . .?

Like an opening flower, the world opens to me;
The forces of nature and mankind I witness.
„The world is tough“, the mother warns;
For tomorrow I strive,
The future . . .?

Franklin M. Chirwa

Prickly Euphorbia raises candelabra branches to the sunset.

Pitani bwino (Goodbye)